Musical Instruments

Violin

By Nick Rebman

level 1 little blue readers

www.littlebluehousebooks.com

Little Blue House is distributed by North Star Editions:
sales@northstareditions.com | 888-417-0195

Produced for Little Blue House by Red Line Editorial.

Photographs ©: Shutterstock Images, cover, 4, 7, 9, 11, 13, 14–15, 17, 19, 21, 23, 24 (top left), 24 (top right), 24 (bottom left), 24 (bottom right)

Library of Congress Control Number: 2022911131

ISBN
978-1-64619-704-0 (hardcover)
978-1-64619-736-1 (paperback)
978-1-64619-797-2 (ebook pdf)
978-1-64619-768-2 (hosted ebook)

Printed in the United States of America
Mankato, MN
012023

About the Author

Nick Rebman is a writer and editor who lives in Minnesota. He enjoys reading, walking his dog, and playing rock songs on his drum set.

Table of Contents

My Violin

I play the violin.

It sounds nice.

I play the violin.

It has four strings.

string

I play the violin.
I hold the bow in my right hand.

bow

I play the violin.
I move the bow across the strings.

I play the violin.
I press the strings with my left hand.

I play the violin.

I have a teacher.

teacher

I play the violin.
I learn to read
sheet music.

sheet music

I play the violin.

I practice in my room.

I play the violin.

I get better and better.

I play the violin.

I am in a band.

band

Glossary

band

sheet music

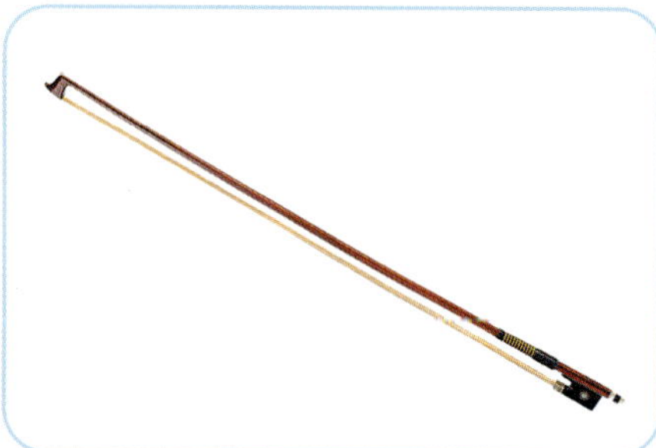

bow

teacher

Index